A Treasury of Poetry for Children

Written By
Johanne Lee

Illustrated by
Alexandra Fowler

INTO THE WILLOW WOOD

Into the Willow Wood Copyright Cornish Books 2024

Published by Cornish Books 2024

All illustration copyright© of Alexandra Fowler 2024. All Text copyright© of Johanne Lee 2024. All rights reserved. No part of this book may be reproduced or transmitted by any means, electronic, mechanical, photocopying or otherwise without the prior permission of the publisher.

Cornish Books

Krowji, Redruth, Cornwall, England, TR15 3AJ

Printed and Distributed in the USA by Bookvault

www.cornishbooks.com

ISBN: 978-1-8384701-8-0

USA Edition

Alternative editions available for worldwide

Dedication

For Elsie

This book is dedicated to all those need a little encouragement to imagine they can -

"You can dream , you can achieve, you can do anything if you believe!"

From Dream Big Little One by Johanne Lee.

A thank you to my parents for the love of reading, my children for inspiring me and my one and only for his support.

A special thank you to family, friends, readers and Maisie for sprinkling me with belief ...

This book will donate all proceeds to the very special Willow Wood Hospice in honour of all the people it has helped and continues to help daily.

I am so proud of this book thank you Alexandra Fowler at Cornish Books for creating the beautiful illustrations and publishing it.

With love

Johanne Lee

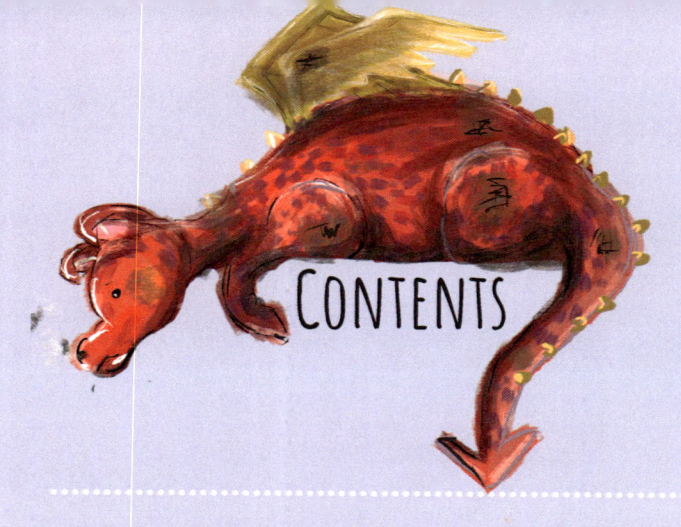

Contents

One Tiny Butterfly 6

But Why 8

When a Dragon Met a King 10

The Sway of the Fickle 14

The Importance of Trees 18

A Quackers Poem 22

Whale Song 24

Never ever feel… 28

Into the Willow Wood 32

Caterpillar 38

The Hare on the Hill	42
The Truth Fairies	44
One Day...	46
Differently Do	48
A Silver Lining	50
The Breath of the Book	52
Conversation with the Moon	56
Books Make...	62
Dear Robin	66
All of the World	68
Positive Poetry Postcards	70

One Tiny Butterfly

One tiny butterfly fluttered of its love
to a ladybird, an earthworm then a witchity grub
a starling heard its murmur
told the blackbird and a dove

Who peacefully passed on the news
to wren and thrush and cat
who didn't pause to congratulate
   then told the hanging bat

What fruit! flapped bat
then flew the news to cave
a passing dolphin splashed its glee
then whispered to each wave

  Oh the whale in breach
  to others reach
  did siren each cetacean
  the turtles twirled
  delighted
  in their surfing whirled formation

    With a gliding fin the shark in grin
    did nudge a jellyfish
    did you hear about the butterfly
    love in its exist

   The octopus trembled
   blushed blue and then pink
   found a stingray who didn't know
   sunk in sea bed think

Who knocked on to a hermit crab
vulnerable of shell
who decided to crawl eastward
tell the elephants as well

As it edged towards the coastline
told the shoal who told the gull
who shrieked upon the skyline
to the clouds who puffed up full

Pitter pattered on the water
echoed far below, thunder raised the lightning
cracked the sky in lit up show

This reminded every tree stumped
who passed on to every leaf
how the butterfly who wished for love
had found its wind beneath

Every wing flew their elation
told each bug and every worm
for in the quiet parts of forestry
a word they hadn't learnt …

One tiny butterfly fluttered wings above
now every ladybird and earthworm
has spread its fluttered love
beyond the lions and the tigers
to the world a curled up bud
to open possibility
and flower something good

But Why

I wish you could be different
said the petal to its leaf
thinner maybe less prickly
less spiny underneath

Now now, said the stem
we grow as we are made
it's not for us to question
foundations planted laid

I wish you were purple
said the leaf to the flower
your insipid pink is pale I think
drab and rather dour

Now now, said the stem
we colour as we will
in every shade is beauty made
I'll not hear you talk ill

I wish you would appreciate
all of what you house
your leaf and its belief
Inner beauty you both espouse

Now now, said the flower and leaf
we hadn't thought beyond fresh air
in future we'll look deep in our dirt
for in growth you've made us aware

When a Dragon met a King

When a dragon met a king
fished for compliments gathering
one a tiny breath of fire
the other now fluttering wing

I crown you, cried the dragon
I'm taller in flaming myth
Ah, said the king
Yet I stand tallest on monolith

Tis but a stone barely touching the sky
I hover in beauty and fearsome I fly
Ah, said the king but I rule the land
Harvest the pickings it's all rather grand

Prosperity precedes me
abundant in rite
to the lizards and the skulking I am swift in flight

Humph! said the dragon I bring change
I transform
I am bold in appearance
far flung from the norm
I am wise I am ancient
All these years I've been patient
I'll raise the bar for you king
I have crowned you under my wing

Ah, said the king it's a plan subtle hatched
It's a deal little dragon for we are certainly well matched

THE SWAY OF THE FICKLE

The fae with the fickle
an ickle black cat

through the land of the nickel
prowled its need to get fat

Come, sang the fae
to the bundle of fur

Paying no heed to
cautionary slur

Together through heather
through weather blown east

Black cat softly purring
to the fae nothing beast

The sprites lit up warnings
great goblets of fright

The moon spoke of dawning
sure as day stole the night

The fae with the fickle
an ickle black cat

An infatuation
It was odd as a fact

By the light of the silvery
alone by the pond

The fae to the fickle
pledged its ickle heart fond

A fur ball was coughed
sent the fae to the air

The teeth of the black cat
were somehow right there

Black cat leapt scratches
to catch break the wings

Of the fae and her fairytales
and sweet happy things

Forlorn of the warnings
tired of fleet flight

Ickle fickle black cat
envisioned cruel delight

He was stronger of claws
In stealth trod his silence

Feline his way toward glassy eyed violence

Fae in a faint of the fickle now a foe

Collapsed midst the copse of the cawing in crow

With his high tailed balance and extraordinary focus

Previously the whiskers of a horrid hocus pocus

He sprang …

Oh the feline left by fickle
yet the fae found the strength

To exert from inert with her very last tenth

Flew into the cats eyes
now seen in their green

And the forest rose sprightly
A spectacular scene

No more the fickle a foe of the fae
the forest closed its doors in a magical way

The leaf sent its lyric
the tree trunk its bark

The sprite startled black cat
and a sting left its mark

The ferns in discern and the growling green ants

Straddled the fickle and its fake friendly stance

Mud blood and greenery
Every stem of the scenery

Fought back!

The fae in defeat of the fickle black cat

Though her heart wore a bandage
and her wings hurt her back

The fickle now friendless fled the fae and forest fleet

The black cat tested luck as it high tailed cross the street

The wheel of life the world and its wife
saw fickle in trickled defeat

For the magic of life isn't the fight or the strife …

                it's the lesson we never repeat

The Importance of Trees

He was the last of a thousand acorns
hybrid of the forests heart
carrying the twine
and the oak of mothered start

He was the last of a thousand sycamore
he carried helicopter hope
rhododendron headaches
and the greenery of old rope

He was the last of a thousand birch
besmirched and whipped lashes
he carried every incident
In creepy crawled flashes

He was the last of a thousand willows
Oh the crickets upped and wept
as the catkins were destroyed
and the batty were bereft

He was the last of a thousand rowan
when he found in curious probe
settled in his palm
a sudden need to save the globe

He was the last of a thousand trees
the solid root of a world turned cutter
and as he braced to sink his roots
It was heard his leaves to mutter

We've been burned scorched torched and maimed
cut down in our prime
traffic tamed
stolen of our forests
saplings and our hedge
stolen of the song in creep to a desperate ledge

I am the last and I must bend with this breeze
In saving the globe
I must replant the seed
There's no carbon copy
of the importance of trees
our leafy revival
or forestry's succeed

Though they shivered disapproval
he'd carried them so long
they prepared to synthesise
strive to mossy strong

He was the last of a thousand borne
the woodland of a past
and as autumn felled a sorry leaf
hope was sudden grasped …

for he was the last

A Quackers Poem

Quack! said Jack a Raven rare and black
the ducks giggled ferociously because only ducks can quack !

Oink! oink! said the bird
parroting each word
birds flew in a frenzy
for this they'd never heard

Neeeeigh! said the cow
who also sometimes said Meow
the horses galloped wildly
while the cat just purred a wow

Mooooo! said the goat and jumped over the fence
landed by the ducks who were confused by the pretence

Woof! said the pig
in charge of fun and games
we can be whoever
sometimes different than our names

The squirrel ran to hide in one of its many huts
and stayed there over winter
for the world it could see was nuts !

Whale Song

There's a lonely whale in the Caribbean Sea
singing by itself a haunting melody

Along came Olive Ridley please may I join in ?
the whale didn't stop singing - so Olive set back off in swim

The melody vibrating waves attracted next a fish
rattled by the humming noise
for silence was its wish

Please could I ask said a clown fish passing by
can I ask why you're singing
can you please tell me why ?

The whale in **full** harmony floating higher notes
reverberating round the sea and **rattling** tender boats

Next along was marlin **knocking** on the whale
can I ask who are you singing to ?
what's the purpose of this tale ?

Some of us are resting, the grunts and porcupine
ask that someone tells you
it's way past singing time

The whale now on its chorus
uninterrupted still
surrounded by the plankton
the damsel and the krill

A passing dolphin bottle nosed
suggests it changed this tune it chose

Out from the dark a pointed nose shark
with grating teeth and tired eye
appeared to ask - still singing ?

Why ?

The drumfish, the snake eel, sting ray and the chub
danced by the whale like an undersea club

Past midnight with delight they danced with the moon
in a mesmerised state to the lonely whales tune

Days later still singing to a wide open sea
an octopus and a ***jellyfish*** try to tickle and sting
but the whale in its blubber thick
continued to sing

Just then out of nowhere
a whoosh splash and breach
the entertainers of the sea
arrived within its reach

Stop singing they tell him
and slowly he agrees he sings for the whales
to reach calmer seas

    Mama humpback and calf
      came to find a warmer breeze
        found their way by listening
          To the whale song of the seas

Never ever feel...

Never ever feel your words are too small
or to climb a rocky alphabet in fear you might fall
see your intention stay curled in a ball
there's always a ladder in small steps crawl

Somewhere there's a tree ripening in space
holding fruits of labours a seed of you in place
somewhere in the gritty earth the beginning of your shoots
taking hold of ideas that quickly grow your roots

Never ever feel your contemplated wish
is swimming in an ocean you'll never ever fish
consider yourself not enough or tall enough to try
for when you're small to climb your dreams
your ceiling is the sky

Somewhere there's a fishing rod
to try and catch your hopes
equipment to go climbing with
for safety on life's slopes
cramp ons, cling ons, arm bands -
hands to throw ropes

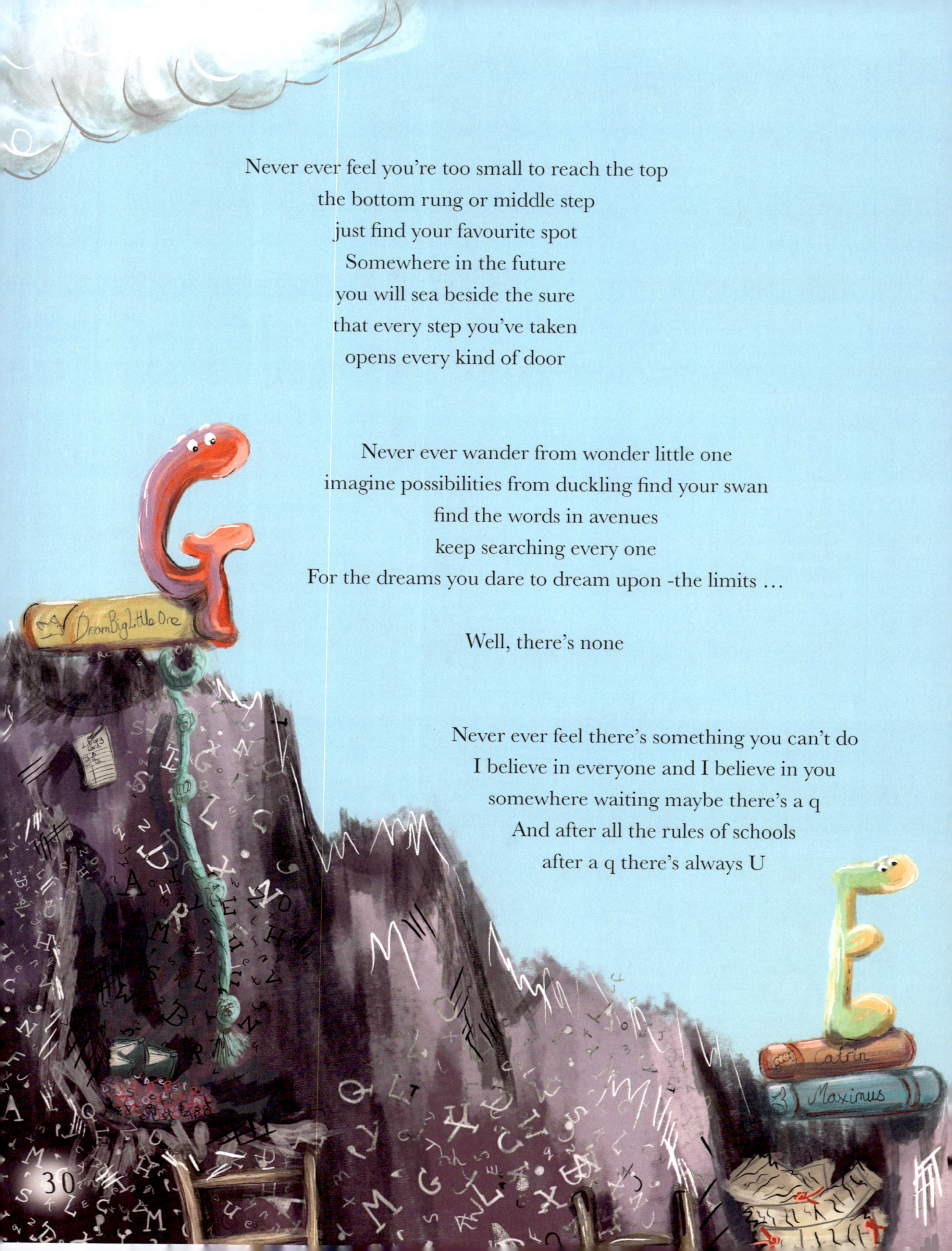

Never ever feel you're too small to reach the top
the bottom rung or middle step
just find your favourite spot
Somewhere in the future
you will sea beside the sure
that every step you've taken
opens every kind of door

Never ever wander from wonder little one
imagine possibilities from duckling find your swan
find the words in avenues
keep searching every one
For the dreams you dare to dream upon -the limits …

Well, there's none

Never ever feel there's something you can't do
I believe in everyone and I believe in you
somewhere waiting maybe there's a q
And after all the rules of schools
after a q there's always U

Never
ever
feel there's something
you can't do

Into the Willow Wood

Willow was scared of the woods, an old tale said all the trees were weeping,
poison Ivy creeping, and ghosts wandered -never sleeping …

Since a child
she had steered well clear of the forest and it's wild

Side by side the trees would hide
all the scary things inside

Once for a dare her friends had gathered there
Into the woods gone prepared
but she too scared … ran home

There were stories of weeping and wailing, things tangled and flailing, friends
had scattered got lost, and little Billy Birch had been touched by a finger of frost

Voices calling
he'd trancelike said
he was falling
then lifted
and ever after was gifted …
with a knowing sight

'always' he kept saying,
'always walk towards the light'

So willow had planted trees of her own
her own garden grown
and though she never planted fear
she had kept the saplings close -and near

How wonderful to grow your family
she loved every branch inevitably
every single leaf a possibility
she'd told them always stand
for each others right to be ...

But lately growing gaunt, growing older
the forests haunt
with their darkening glance
she felt she was being called
towards the entrance

roots being pulled, though she fought and she fought
the pull was too strong

and that's how willow found a new belong

The trees she once had spied
thinking scary things inside

all their branches opened wide

all the tales and myths had lied

The willows weren't weeping
they had burst from bark in elation
created an umbrella
to house the earth in celebration

The ivy in trails of curling creep
cuddled each tree in a hug
that a ladder be climbed from the smallest on earth
to reach treetops and the height of their love

Ghosts were smiling sprites
sparkling and shimmering bright
dancing a trail

A sign post towards a beautiful light

All manner of spectacle
were happy and free
there were lilies and bluebells
like a wide open sea

The lyric of the nightingale
chatters with the wren
willow left her earthly state
and flew towards them

Seeing an old friend
a great silver truncated church
in the centre of the forestry
there ...was Billy Birch

You can go home -sighed the oak
take a moments respite
But willow was tired
and the forests delight

  couldn't be matched

    Her eyes opening opened to the far and wide
    to a feeling of peace
    beyond all she'd ever tried

    Her leaves returned
    she saw the forest anew
    she grew so tall
    trying to peep through

      and say I'm home -

Find me where the bluebells grow
the Ivy clings
the squirrels burrow
and she grew in renew
like a giant hello

A clever little leaf
that had fallen sprung anew
saw the willow peeping
and how the forest changed in view

Something of its ancestry
a song midst the trees
the chatter of a grandmother
whispered on the breeze

Where the willow wept -said one
where the Ivy its perfume clings
where myth speaks of the dying
and gathering their wings

But the willow grew taller
and the forest opened wide
inviting others to its paradise
its sanctuary inside

The silver birch reminded
what's given returns something good
and ever after to spend time at peace
they went into the willow wood

CATERPILLAR

Caterpillar caterpillar
its nearly afternoon!

Caterpillar caterpillar
come out from your cocoon

You've slept through the birds in chirp
the bees in buzzing pride

The ladybird who climbed your branch
and tried to peep inside

I saw another caterpillar
that waved and didn't hide

Caterpillar caterpillar
the eve of night arrives

Caterpillar caterpillar
the bees all in their hives !

The owl is sending wit to woo
bats in a flap fly circles round you

Hedgehogs brave a prickly walk
the feline purr in meowing stalk

I waited all night
saw the first breath of light

At the leaving of the moon
began the breaking of cocoon

I waited caterpillar and now I'm asking why

you

never said

you were

leaving

And who's this

BUTTERFLY?

The Hare on the Hill

A lonesome hare
sat waiting on yonder hill
The sun smiled at him daily
the moon it's light did spill

Yet still a lonely hare nods at passers by
Something about his quiet stance
does catch the thoughtful eye

Chance awaits a meeting
the hare seemed sure of fate
sat stoic in its loneliness
a long and quiet wait

The rabbit came and asked anew
as many passing did
pray speak of what this hill does hold
What magic in it hid ?

The hare always a pleasant chap
a kind and gentle face
This hill shall be the meeting
where my love shall find its place

The rabbit raised a quizzical brow
'and when was this arranged?'
Hare replied 'Tis nothing fixed -the message mixed
from here we were estranged'

The rabbit hopped to friends scoffed
What madness! a fool
on the hill
He waits for love somehow estranged
Ne'er met, perhaps he's ill-

For years the elements tried in kind
to shield his sorry stance
For lonely as he seemed to be
he oft was seen to dance

The years in wait crumbled his gait
his dance began to slow
His eyes still smiled his face in kind
threw seeds in flowering know

The sun this day was ever warm
A sky in cloudless blue

The hare with hope still born of faith
Saw love to life come true

No more the lonely sight forlorn
The hill turned quiet of will
The sun plays shade on the spot he prayed

Where a shadow of his faith- lingers still

The Truth Fairies

Mum was pretending to be a fairy
changing a tooth for a pound
Mum was pretending to be a fairy
as if there's no fairies around

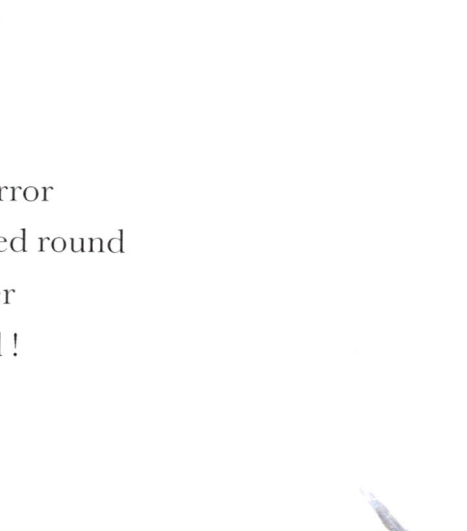

Throwing glitter about the place
Sending little letters and notes
The tooth fairies couldn't believe it
were furious and mighty provoked

Mum was pretending to be a fairy
the flowers and their fairies were cross
They joined together with the fairies with the feathers
and the Sylph like ones from the moss

They tied a string of teeth to mums mirror
they sprinkled her with dust they carried round
They covered her in daisies and heather
and they lifted her clean off the ground !

Mum was in a dream like state
She was sure she had a temperature, felt ill
She was high off the ground seeing fairies and their pounds
and teeth that had never seen a drill

The fairies flew her across the town
showed her how fairies feel
Prodded her to rethink -tickled her 'til she was pink'

'Fairies' they said 'are real !'

One Day

One day a star was called to earth
to travel where the waters birth
goodbye to skies said little star
long wondered and wished on from places afar

It was dark in voyage to land on two feet
grow two hands a smile to meet
giant moonbeam and a galaxy await
for the star long wished upon
a love to recreate -

Differently Do

You weren't born to be the same
surely you can your differences see
each part of you that puzzles
creates a startling intensity
of follicle and chemicals
great rivers flow the vein
mesmerised miraculous
delectable domain
there you were speaking ordinary
diminishing fabulous flame
these quiet disguises still surprises…

for you weren't born to be the same

A Silver Lining

Pitter patter raindrops from a pocket in the sky
A giant in an overcoat had let his treasure fly

    Pennies shimmered lightning
    golf balls hailing down
    a locket from a relative and one gold crown

    Footsteps bellowed thunder
    raced along with clouds
    frowning of the blunder
    for giants weren't allowed
    to hoard the past in pockets
    take pennies from the ground
    and hoard them where the atmosphere
    has plenty glitter found

Pity from the pattered being splattered by the change
raining cats and silver dogs
golf balls filling drains, gathering the lockets and finding golden crown
to pile upon the causeway
at the entrance to the town

    The giant was so grateful
    all the treasure in a mound
    with hands in grit and gravel
    placed his treasure in the ground
    stitching up the pocket rained all knick knacks on the crowd
    then he sewed as thanks a silver lining -into every cloud

The Breath of the Book

Once upon a time a dragon lived in a favourite book
breathing fiery words to delighted eyes
climbed imaginations mountains
and burst through pages in surprise
he was held, he was heard
to those listening to his words
but then came speedy sounds
verse left on skates
and the books were forgotten
because nobody could narrate ...

The dragon thrust into pages of dust
high on the shelves
with the fairies and elves
the myths and old stories
forgotten in their glories

An interested squirrel now stood by the libraries door
Without a key
and of words a bit unsure
Out came the alphabet a giant of many vowels
booming out great consonants
letters wise like owls

But I can't read …said the squirrel in its own way
Out popped a giant sound
We begin with letter A -

An old blind mouse limped inside
Open up the books, he said
Our adventures bound in pride

*I've scurried over bumpy trail
to find the stories said in braille
characters are housed within
Sat patiently waiting for ears listening -*

    Off into the library
    what waits he thought for me

        The giant and the heroes and the fairies and the elves
        Blew sprinkling dust from high on their shelves
        the dragon huffed no fire came out -
        But the squirrel said *hey what's this book about* ?
        And the dragon cried great tears of gold
        Because it had waited so long for its story to be told

            I'll help you, said the dragon
            and shouted to the shelves
            Come down! he said to fairies who linked their arms with elves
            Finally some interest in stories and our words -

                *I flew the skies in breath of fire
                This fairy here magic inspired
                This ship it sailed the seven seas
                and dust was sprinkled that all believed -*

*Hope began on chapter one
and we lay upon these pages
but the people were all gone*

The library closed and we never spoke
and the language of the alphabet
Well that was heart broke
In every word and pictured tale
something he said to learn
And from him burst a fiery flame
As interest sparkled in return -

By candlelight most nights it seems
The dragon flies in full glory
Into the heads of the sleepy and their dreams
And tomorrow brings us all another story

Conversation with the Moon

What's it like to see everything?
asked the child of the moon
shining its luminary
where none would assume
it was sad
the moon in quiet repose
of the child's suppose
It was glad

For it was shiny and bright
whereas the dark had covered night
in its disguise
and who can see anything-
asked the child
Of the moons eyes
without you?

Craters looking pin prick
yet giant wide awake
and it's dark side where all its aches hide
were all its tears and heartbreak

It had seen a shooting star
falling too far
getting only one take
And then cut -
the show was over
and the moon was sudden sliced
spliced in its eclipse
Into cavities and craters
had its feelings sadly slipped
to find peace

Oh wintering moon
in ever frowning crease
would the world ever cease
from its darkness

What's it like to feel everything in the universe? said the child
mindful of the hour
and the threat to the wild
two hoots an owl
as the moon in reappear
to the night mooned in scowl

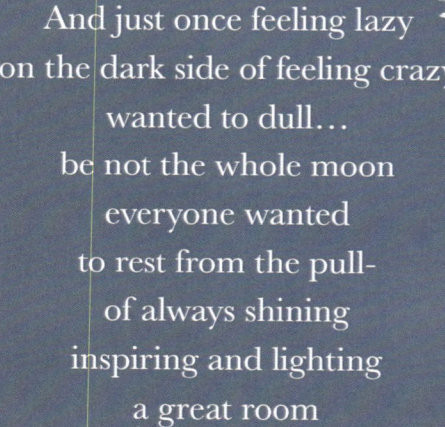

And just once feeling lazy
on the dark side of feeling crazy
wanted to dull…
be not the whole moon
everyone wanted
to rest from the pull-
of always shining
inspiring and lighting
a great room

Taken for granted
Oh wintering moon

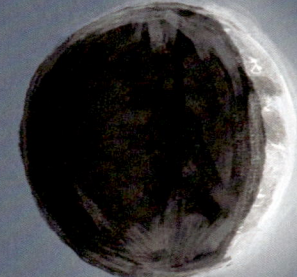

it grows cold

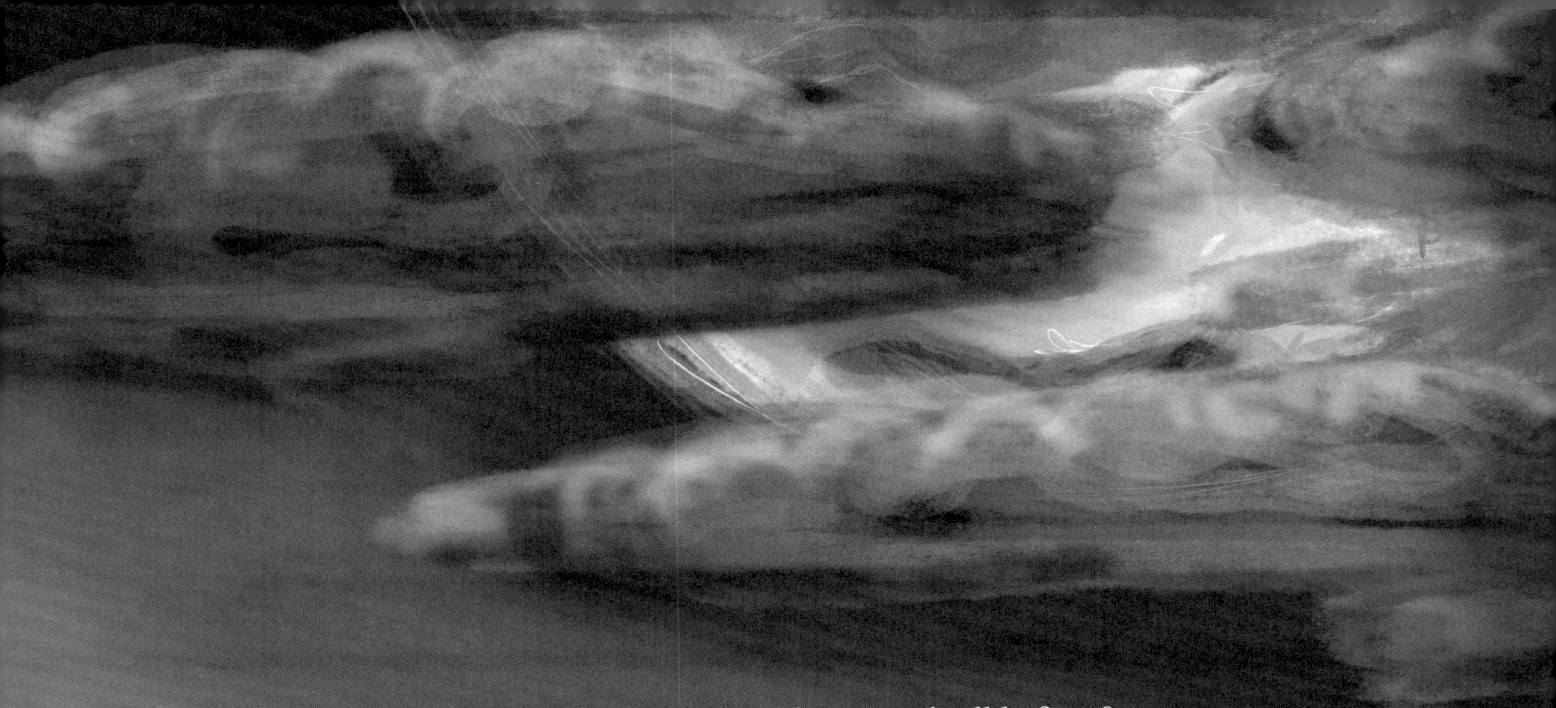

What's it like to know everything, seen it all before ?
said the child from earths core
and carpeted floor
where autumns lost
invaded the meadows
seen a covering of frost
all the skies bossed
and moods of each year

What's it like? said the moon
in the darkness up here
while everyone stares

Well nothing prepares
you for the dearth
of shining a light upon earth
and though your diamond lit eyes
see all the magical inside
I see what looms and is denied
to the stars
and Milky Way
of what my heart can safely say
is sore …

And there are days when the weight of it
I wish to shine no more

until I see -

Hope looks at me
for answers
midst the sky of twinkling dancers
I have to be -

The silver shimmering moon
shines a light
holds a torch
Into the midst of forests loom
gumiserrvi across the sea
shine on harvest endlessly
strikes a chord feeds sonata
On the rivers running free

So I smile

and I pretend

So that every child down there
will know it has **one** friend

will ever stay -
shine a smile and curl a care
that never goes away

BOOKS MAKE...

Books make great towers
fill full many hours
drive imaginations
on page coached to destinations
north, south to the west of east
where the grumbling tums of brains eat, feast
on giant peach and sugared plum
and pirates prose in drizzled rum

        Books make great dominoes
        stand in rows where diction flows
        and lead us down a magic path
        where elves, imps and ogres laugh
        and where the forest harbours trust
        in tiny leaves of fairies dust
        their iron lore won't ever rust

Books make great love seats
rip up time with their great feats
romancing enchanting in mystery keep dancing
where sleuths stealthily research
solve and sniffer search
for just another turn of page
transported to a different age

Books make great arm rests
foot rests and treasure chests
piles and piles can stretch for miles
in windows awhile
head height in smiles
make ideas named
in new pastures framed
where secrets and intrigue
are intricate trained

Books make great trains
in chew chewed over thought
down and around all the tracks being sought
up in the attic they turn on the light
of mayhem and magical
and tantalised fright
from boardroom and picture

lines won't restrict you

Books make great towers
tales of cities and tumbleweed towns
building great brain cells
intelligence crowns
they save you from screens
whilst screaming of dreams
hold tight your heart
whilst painting life's art
with wait a minute words …
towering trees
full of birdsong and birds

Books make great doors
In planks they write floors
in stone they scribe laws
in crackpot find flaws
with handles of brass, door knockers bold
they bang on the ear drums
a story be told
closed on idea they open, reveal
a house we conceal
full of kitchens that feel
a warm boiling need
to kettle on and read

Books make great boats
sail somewhere remote
write you the captain
of adventure get soaked
ring a bell on entry to ports that provoke
harbour the steps that reach understand
Books great companions
to wander in hand
and speak to the mind
books make great towers
to cling on and climb

Dear Robin

We must take care of the red breast
said chiff chaff to the wren
and barn owl could barely pretend
he wasn't listening one ear cocked again

'Why, said the sparrow, I am starved'
the crows crowd and jackdaw thieves
the blackbirds ever sing arrival
its red breast the seasons retrieves

With puffed up chest
and jaunty appeal
but really all this flapping about
does nothing to conceal
our decline
there's murmurations
we fade of time

Clipped wings won't fly
I wonder if they'll notice
when there's no song in the sky ?

And that's what redbreast overheard
wrenched and hurt began to cry

Such a flurry to comfort familiar
the wind sent a tickle from the breeze
chiff chaff chirped he'd found some seed

As robins aching reddening heart …
wondered how love it could feed

All of the World

All of the world
in a hug dare we dream
that the stars will make friends
with the planets being mean

And the moon in a smirk
looking sly at the sky
can we just for a moment
let bygones float by

Oh this galaxy of mixed up
the dark swamping light
yet the peep of resilience
shining solid bright

What meteoric advancement
if we all could be friends
spaced out I know
but could we all make amends ?

Little comets of our existence
break free of the black hole
bring us light years from warring
into kind kindred souls

Send love into orbit
let Venus meet Mars
and hold life universal
as precious as the stars

Exquisite in ethos
to each other the earth
how simple the world seems
understanding its worth

Positive Poetry Postcards

Before launching into the enchanting world of 'Into the Willow Wood,' we invited children all over the UK to craft vibrant poetry postcards inspired by Johannes' thought-provoking poem 'But Why.'

With its inherent lessons, 'But Why' sparks conversation about embracing differences. We asked these young poets to infuse their postcards with the essence of kindness, echoing the theme of Johannes' poem.

Johanne understands the vital role of nurturing poetry creation as a form of creativity and expression, particularly from a young age. Encouraging this artistic endeavor is paramount. That's why we made sure that seeing their work in print for the first time was a part of the prize. It's a momentous occasion for any budding poet. As we embarked on the journey toward the launch of 'Into the Willow Wood,' we saw it as an opportunity not just to celebrate Johannes' enchanting poetry but also to foster a love for creative expression in children across the UK. And what better way to do so than by showcasing their heartfelt words and illustrations in our book?

The winning entry not only earned its place in the book but also received its own illustration.

Turn the page to revel in our champion's creation.

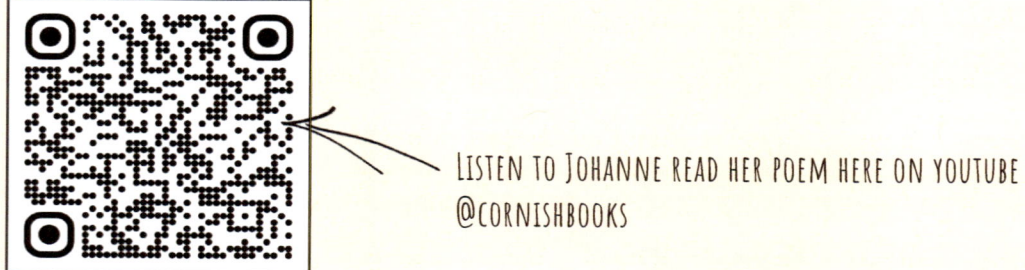

Listen to Johanne read her poem here on youtube
@cornishbooks

To   Everyone
_____
_____
_____
_____
_____

A Positive Postcard

Be yourself because nobody can say you're doing it wrong. If you don't like the road you're walking on, start paving another one.

Kindness is one thing you can give away, but it will always come back. Smiling is contagious, once you give it away it will spread.

Jake S
Kennall Vale School

About the Author

Johanne Lee, is a proud Mancunian mother of 3, poet and author of 7 children's picture books.

She has personally written two collections of poetry, 'Womans Journey', and 'Under the lavender moon', as part of the Open Skies Spotlight series as well as embarking on one joint collection with Debbie Clewer called 'Pieces of Hope'.

Johanne's poetry has also gained recognition within the wider poetry community, and she has been published in over 30 anthologies. These include Jimmy Broccoli's 'Spotlight Anthology', the sacred feminine 1-3, southern Arizona press, wheelsong 2, Impspired magazine and DPS Ezine to name a few.

With her children's books, Johanne has guest featured on the Twinkl podcast, discussing raising awareness of sustainability in early years, and enjoys inspiring children through her visits to schools.

All books raise for various charities and hope to raise awareness of subjects close to her heart and hopefully yours.

She can be found as **@Johanneleeauthor** on Facebook and Instagram.

www.ingramcontent.com/pod-product-compliance
Lightning Source LLC
Chambersburg PA
CBRC091504220426
43661CB00022B/1311